That's Not
CAN I HAV
GIRAFFE?

By Bert Wilberforce

Gareth Stevens
PUBLISHING

Please visit our website, www.garethstevens.com. For a free color catalog of all our high-quality books, call toll free 1-800-542-2595 or fax 1-877-542-2596.

Library of Congress Cataloging-in-Publication Data

Names: Wilberforce, Bert, author.
Title: Can I have a pet giraffe? / Bert Wilberforce.
Description: New York : Gareth Stevens Publishing, [2019] | Series: That's not a pet! | Includes index.
Identifiers: LCCN 2017040516| ISBN 9781538217924 (library bound) | ISBN 9781538217948 (pbk.) | ISBN 9781538217955 (6 pack)
Subjects: LCSH: Giraffe–Juvenile literature. | Pets–Juvenile literature.
Classification: LCC QL737.U56 W57 2018 | DDC 599.638–dc23
LC record available at https://lccn.loc.gov/2017040516

First Edition

Published in 2019 by
Gareth Stevens Publishing
111 East 14th Street, Suite 349
New York, NY 10003

Copyright © 2019 Gareth Stevens Publishing

Editor: Therese Shea
Designer: Sarah Liddell

Photo credits: Cover, p. 1 mariait/Shutterstock.com; p. 5 E. O./Shutterstock.com; p. 7 PHOTOCREO Michal Bednarek/Shutterstock.com; p. 9 Matej Hudovernik/Shutterstock.com; pp. 11, 24 (horns) Cathy Withers-Clarke/Shutterstock.com; p. 13 wanida tubtawee/Shutterstock.com; pp. 15, 24 (tongue) Nagel Photography/Shutterstock.com; p. 17 Phonlaphat/Shutterstock.com; p. 19 Kathy Kay/Shutterstock.com; p. 21 Pyty/Shutterstock.com; p. 23 Sunychka Sol/Shutterstock.com.

All rights reserved. No part of this book may be reproduced in any form without permission in writing from the publisher, except by a reviewer.

Printed in the United States of America

CPSIA compliance information: Batch #CS18GS: For further information contact Gareth Stevens, New York, New York at 1-800-542-2595.

Contents

A Tall Pet? 4

Giraffe Bodies 8

Eating and Drinking 16

Too Tall! 20

Words to Know 24

Index 24

I want a pet.
I want a giraffe!

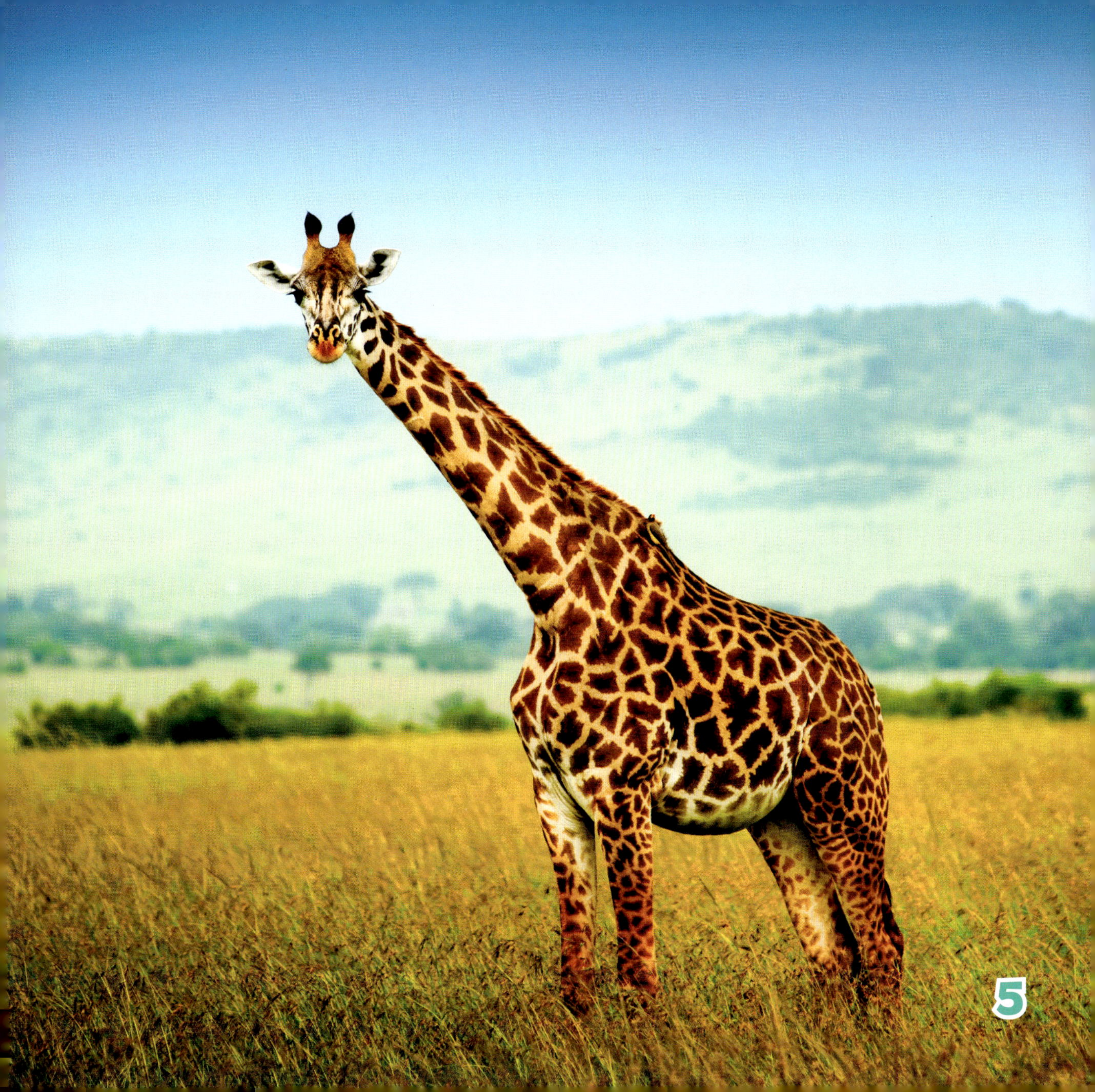

Giraffes are the tallest animals!
They live in Africa.

7

They have long legs and a long neck.

9

Some have two horns.

11

Giraffes have spots.
They might help
them hide!

13

They have a long tongue.
It's black, blue, or purple!

15

They eat plants.
They eat leaves off trees.

17

Giraffes need to spread their legs to drink water! It's hard to reach!

19

Giraffes aren't good pets. They're too tall!

21

I can visit them at the zoo!

23

Words to Know

horns

tongue

Index

Africa 6
horns 10
legs 8, 18

neck 8
spots 12
tongue 14